DEFINING EVENTS
of the Twenty-First Century

SOCIAL CHANGE

in the Twenty-First Century

by Bethany Bryan

ReferencePoint
Press®

San Diego, CA

LIBRARY OF CONGRESS CATALOGING-IN-PUBLICATION DATA

Names: Bryan, Bethany.
Title: Social change in the twenty-first century / Bethany Bryan.
Description: San Diego, CA : ReferencePoint Press, Inc., [2020] | Series:
    Defining events of the twenty-first century | Audience: Grade 9 to 12. |
    Includes bibliographical references and index.
Identifiers: LCCN 2019000786 (print) | LCCN 2019002995 (eBook) | ISBN
    9781682826089 (eBook) | ISBN 9781682826072 (hardcover)
Subjects: LCSH: Social history--21st century--Juvenile literature. | Social
    change--United States--Juvenile literature. | Women's rights--United
    States--History--21st century--Juvenile literature. | Sexual minorities--United
    States--History--21st century--Juvenile literature.
Classification: LCC HN18.3 (eBook) | LCC HN18.3 .B79 2020 (print) | DDC
    306--dc23
LC record available at https://lccn.loc.gov/2019000786

CONTENTS

IMPORTANT EVENTS

2001
Religious extremists hijack four planes and crash them into the two towers of the World Trade Center, the Pentagon, and a field near Shanksville, Pennsylvania.

2014
Malala Yousafzai wins the Nobel Peace Prize for her activism in equality in education for girls.

2012
Seventeen-year-old Trayvon Martin is murdered by George Zimmerman.

2014
Michael Brown is killed by police in the Saint Louis suburb of Ferguson, Missouri.

2009
Dr. George Tiller is murdered by an anti-abortion fanatic in Wichita, Kansas.

2000   2002   2004   2006   2008

2008
Barack Obama is elected the first African American president.

2011
The Syrian military opens fire on peaceful protesters, leading to outbreak of civil war. The conflict creates a large number of refugees, and the policies surrounding these displaced people become a point of controversy.

"I WILL STAND WITH THE MOST VULNERABLE"

JOIN US • LOVEARMY.ORG

NO BAN NO WALL

2015
Hillary Clinton announces that she's running for president in 2016.

2016
The US Supreme Court hears the case of Jack Phillips, who refused in 2012 to make a cake for a gay couple's wedding reception.

2015
Caitlyn Jenner comes out as transgender, one of the first high-profile trans women to do so.

2018
Christine Blasey Ford testifies before the Senate that Supreme Court nominee Brett Kavanaugh sexually assaulted her in the 1980s.

2010   2012   2014   2016   2018

2015
The US Supreme Court strikes down state-level bans on same-sex marriage, effectively legalizing it across the country.

2016
The first so-called "bathroom bill" is passed into law in North Carolina.

2016
Donald Trump is elected forty-fifth president of the United States.

2017
Multiple women accuse movie mogul Harvey Weinstein of sexual assault and harassment, launching the #MeToo movement.

5

Black Lives Matter in America

On the evening of February 26, 2012, in a home in Sanford, Florida, a suburb of Orlando, the TV was tuned to the NBA All-Star Game. Seventeen-year-old Trayvon Martin was there visiting his dad, Tracy, after some issues at school had resulted in a ten-day suspension. Martin decided to run out for some snacks and headed to a nearby convenience store wearing a gray hoodie pulled up to protect him from the light rain. At the store, he bought a bag of candy and an iced tea and then left. The store's footage of the purchase recorded some of the last moments of Martin's life.

Nearby, Sanford resident George Zimmerman had noticed Martin walking around the neighborhood. Zimmerman was captain of the local neighborhood watch program and called 911 to report suspicious behavior. "This guy looks like he's up to no good or he's on drugs or something," said Zimmerman to the dispatcher.[1]

Martin was on the phone with his girlfriend, Rachel Jeantel, as he headed back to the house where he was staying. He noticed he was being followed by an SUV. Jeantel listened as Martin confronted the man driving the vehicle—Zimmerman. "Why are you following me for?" asked Martin, according to Jeantel's account.[2] Then she heard sounds of a struggle and screams for help, although she could not absolutely identify Martin's voice in her later testimony. By then neighbors had called 911. Zimmerman fired a single shot from a handgun, hitting Martin in the chest. When police arrived, Martin lay facedown on the grass, fatally wounded from the gunshot.

When questioned, Zimmerman insisted that he had fired in self-defense. He said Martin had attacked him, knocking him to the ground and injuring his nose and the back of his head, which were bleeding when he was taken to the police station. After speaking to police, Zimmerman was allowed to go home.

> **"This guy looks like he's up to no good or he's on drugs or something."**[1]
>
> *– George Zimmerman in his call to 911*

News of the incident spread rapidly across the internet. Martin's parents started an online petition calling for Zimmerman to face charges. People began to take notice and spread the word about the petition. Helped along by several celebrities who had taken an interest and posted about the situation on social media, the number of signatures quickly climbed to 2.2 million. People were angry, especially in the black community. Martin had been unarmed. He hadn't been engaging in any criminal activity. Many people believed this was a case of racial profiling—when someone is suspected of wrongdoing because of their race. Had Zimmerman not aggressively confronted him, many felt that Martin would still be alive.

Finally, six weeks after the shooting, prosecutors announced that Zimmerman would be facing charges of second-degree murder and manslaughter in the death of Martin. Hope for justice flooded in for many Americans the next year, as prosecution proceedings in the

Activists called for justice in the aftermath of Martin's death. Their protests would later evolve into the Black Lives Matter movement.

trial against Zimmerman began on June 24, 2013. Others were angry because they felt that Zimmerman's response was justified as an act of self-defense.

On July 13, the jury entered the courtroom to deliver the verdict. George Zimmerman had been acquitted of all charges. Because of the divisive nature of the case, reactions were mixed. In the black community, 86 percent showed disapproval for the verdict, while there was only a 31 percent disapproval rate among whites. Many of those who opposed the verdict showed up to protests around the country. People chanted, "I am Trayvon Martin," and "No justice, no peace."[3] They wore hoodies in solidarity.

Starting a Social Movement

"It was as if we had all been punched in the gut," said Alicia Garza.[4] Garza had been watching the news with friends at a bar in Oakland, California, when the verdict was read. Not only was she disappointed in the verdict, she was disappointed in the public's reaction to it and how many had blamed Martin for his own death. Garza went on Facebook and wrote a long post to express her feelings. She wanted people to come together in the understanding that "black lives matter."[5] A friend of Garza's, Patrisse Cullors, added a

> **"It was as if we had all been punched in the gut."[4]**
>
> *– Activist Alicia Garza in response to the acquittal of George Zimmerman*

hashtag, and the #BlackLivesMatter movement was born. Around the country, people shared the hashtag on social media, reminding their followers that the lives of black individuals should not be dismissed or minimized.

Martin's death could have been lost to time, filed away among other similar cases and forgotten. But because of people who demanded social change, it wasn't. Society is constantly changing. Individually, people are always learning and adapting. They're faced with new challenges and experiences. Social change on a larger scale occurs when enough people go through these changes to alter society as a whole. In the first decades of the twenty-first century, many of these significant changes have already begun to take place. Shifting patterns in attitudes, beliefs, and awareness have affected women, people of color, members of the LGBTQ community, and those who practice religion both in America and abroad.

Chapter 1

How Have Race Relations Changed in America?

The United States has a long history of racial tension, starting with the European explorers and colonists who arrived in North America starting in the 1500s. Indigenous peoples already lived throughout the continent. The colonists displaced, enslaved, or killed vast numbers of indigenous people. This treatment led to outbreaks of violence and bloodshed that continued for centuries and wiped out entire civilizations of native people.

Some of the earliest African slaves in America were brought to the Jamestown Colony, in what is now Virginia, in 1619. Over the next two centuries, 12.5 million slaves were brought to the American colonies, the Caribbean, and South America. Slavery was officially outlawed by the Thirteenth Amendment in 1865. However, discrimination against black people in the United States was far from over. The country remained a dangerous place for former slaves, their descendants, and other people of color.

The late nineteenth century and early twentieth century ushered in what is known as the Jim Crow era. During this time, state laws—commonly called Jim Crow laws—were passed to enforce racial segregation. The laws prohibited white and African American children

White European colonists brought enslaved black Africans to North America in the early 1600s. Slavery remained a major driver of the economy in the southern United States until the 1860s.

from attending the same schools and black people from using the same transportation and occupying the same public spaces as white people. Leaders of the civil rights movement of the 1950s and 1960s—including Martin Luther King Jr., John Lewis, Dorothy Height, and others—pushed back against Jim Crow laws and worked toward federal legislation that would outlaw discrimination. The passage of the Civil Rights Act of 1964, which banned such segregation, seemed to many like a long-awaited first step toward American equality. But the nation remains divided over race issues.

The conflicts that perpetuate these issues aren't limited to American shores. Over the last decade, conflicts have erupted overseas and displaced people from South Sudan, Afghanistan, and Syria, among other nations. A Syrian civil war started in 2011, resulting in the deaths of hundreds of thousands of Syrians. Millions more fled the country, many seeking safety in Europe and the United States. There were 25.4 million refugees worldwide in 2018, and of these, 3.1 million were asylum seekers. These people have fled their home countries and applied to be taken in and protected by a host nation. But finding a welcoming host nation isn't easy. Many people in potential host nations view those from nations in the Middle East and South Asia as a threat to national security because of past acts of terrorism committed by people from those regions. The terrorist attacks of September 11, 2001, were committed by Muslim extremists, and some people wrongly assume that all Muslims share extremist views. This misconception has ushered in an era of xenophobia, racism, and acts of violence against refugees, immigrants, and nonwhite American citizens. In the United States, certain government policies have tightened security, making it more difficult for refugees to seek asylum. According to 2018 numbers from the Pew Research Center, 13 million Syrians have been displaced by the civil war. Although the United States has historically been a welcoming country to refugees, bringing in more than 3 million people since 1980, it only settled 33,000 refugees in 2017, down from 97,000 the previous year.

Today, the United States continues to struggle with racial unrest and issues of discrimination. Since the beginning of the twenty-first century, a number of events have occurred that have fanned the flames of racism in America and heightened the visibility of white

Some people have protested the refugee-blocking policies of the administration of President Donald Trump. They reject the notion that refugees represent a potential danger to the country.

supremacy, an ideology that many thought was firmly in America's past. Social media outlets like Twitter, Facebook, and Reddit help to spread these ideas, making hope and progress seem farther away for those who have always believed that a life in America means a promise of freedom.

The Growth of Racial Tension in the Twenty-First Century

Racism and racial tension continue to thrive in America. They show up on the nightly news, on the internet, and in neighborhoods across the country. But how can a country like the United States, whose founders spoke of seeking individual freedom and liberty, carry such a legacy of discrimination and pain? Many believe that racism is actively passed down from generation to generation. Others, like Jennifer Richeson, a social psychologist from Yale University, believe that racism is learned from the culture as a whole. "The truth is that unless parents actively teach kids not to be racists, they will be. This is not the product of some deep-seated, evil heart that is cultivated," she said in 2017. "It comes from the environment, the air all around us."[6]

> **"This is not the product of some deep-seated, evil heart that is cultivated. It comes from the environment, the air all around us."[6]**
>
> *– Jennifer Richeson, Yale University*

Particular outbursts of racism are often fueled by sudden change or by tragedy, and several such events took place in the early decades of the twenty-first century in the United States.

One of these events occurred on September 11, 2001. That morning, nineteen men, who would later be identified as Muslim extremists, hijacked four airliners soon after they departed from airports on the East Coast. With their destinations in California, each aircraft carried a heavy load of fuel. The terrorists crashed two of the planes into the twin World Trade Center towers in New York City. The impact and subsequent explosion and fire damaged the buildings enough that they then collapsed. A total of 2,753 people, including firefighters and law enforcement personnel, were killed in the New York attacks. The hijackers flew the third plane into the exterior of the Pentagon in Washington, DC, where 184 people were killed. The fourth hijacked plane crashed in a field outside of Shanksville,

Pennsylvania, killing forty onboard. The passengers, who had become aware of the other attacks, attempted to retake control from the terrorists, and the plane went down in the chaos. Responsibility for the attacks was soon attributed to the terrorist group al-Qaeda and its leader Osama bin Laden, a Saudi extremist who had been responsible for bombings of US embassies in Kenya and Tanzania in 1998.

This day was life-changing in a number of ways for Americans. There were survivors directly impacted by the attacks on the World Trade Center and the Pentagon. Others experienced the loss of a loved one, a job, a sense of stability, or their health. But many Americans who were not so closely involved also faced life-changing consequences. After September 11, polls showed that 58 percent of Americans were afraid for their personal safety and the safety of their friends and family. Younger generations had never experienced this level of fear and uncertainty. Never in their lifetimes had so many Americans died through such carefully orchestrated means. How did this happen? What if it happened again?

Fear is a powerful thing—both on a personal level and for a nation reeling in the aftermath of a large-scale terrorist attack. Suspicion was on the rise, and because the attackers had been Muslim, some people began targeting ordinary American Muslims—or even those who just looked as though they might be Muslim. In the year 2000, twelve attacks on Muslim individuals were reported to the Federal Bureau of Investigation (FBI). That number rose to ninety-three in 2001. President George W. Bush was quick to speak out against violence against Muslims. He said in a speech at the Islamic Center of Washington, DC, on September 17, 2001, "America counts millions of Muslims amongst our citizens, and Muslims make an incredibly valuable contribution to our country. Muslims are doctors, lawyers, law professors, members of the military, entrepreneurs, shopkeepers, moms and dads. And they need to be treated with respect. In our anger and emotion, our fellow Americans must treat each other with respect."[7] But his words were not enough to halt discrimination and violence across the country. Muslims continue to be the targets of bias.

A second event that had a significant impact on racial dynamics in the United States was the election of President Barack Obama in 2008. In the years after the September 11 attacks, many Americans looked to political leaders to give them hope and to show them signs of progress. Illinois senator Barack Obama seemed to fit the bill, and on Election Day, he made history, defeating Senator John McCain to become the forty-fourth president of the United States—and the first African American to hold the office. Many people took his win as a sign that the United States was moving forward into what some called a "post-racial" era. In this new world, some people felt, the rise of an African American man into the nation's highest office meant that racism would fade away.

> "Muslims are doctors, lawyers, law professors, members of the military, entrepreneurs, shopkeepers, moms and dads. And they need to be treated with respect."[7]
>
> – President George W. Bush, September 17, 2001

However, this hopeful notion did not come to pass. While many Americans who disagreed with Obama felt that way on the basis of politics, others objected to his race. Some of the reactions were violent or threatening in nature. In the days leading up to the election, on the University of Kentucky's Lexington campus, a likeness of

Barack Obama was found hanging from a tree. This was a reminder of a terrible chapter of US history in which more than 4,000 lynchings of black Americans were recorded between 1877 and 1950 throughout the United States. After the election, reports of racist activity continued to surface across the country. In Hardwick, New Jersey, and Apolacan Township, Pennsylvania, Obama supporters reported finding burning crosses on their lawns, a reminder of a time in the late 1800s and early 1900s when a racist group called the Ku Klux Klan (KKK) terrorized African Americans, other people of color, and their allies. Racial slurs and death threats against the president-elect were frequently spotted as the nation drew closer to Inauguration Day. Social media services such as Facebook and Twitter were relatively new and played a big part in the Obama campaign. But during and after the election, many also used these social media platforms to share racist memes, false information, and conspiracy theories. Hate was growing, and many felt powerless to stop it.

Michael Brown and Ferguson

Violence carried out by police against black Americans received widespread attention in the 2010s, driving the Black Lives Matter movement and spurring activists to make demands for change. Among the most impactful of these incidents was the killing of Michael Brown. Brown was eighteen years old when he was killed in a confrontation with police officer Darren Wilson on August 9, 2014, in the Saint Louis, Missouri, suburb of Ferguson. Brown was walking down the street with a friend when Wilson pulled up beside them and asked Brown to step over to the sidewalk. Wilson said later he believed that Brown was potentially involved in a robbery that had taken place earlier in the day.

The precise details of what happened next may never be known for sure. After the incident, Wilson insisted that an enraged Brown grabbed for his gun, forcing Wilson to react with deadly force. Wilson fired a total of twelve shots, seven of which hit Brown. Eyewitness accounts provided conflicting information, with some insisting that Brown was surrendering and others stating that they saw him attack the officer. Some, including the friend who was with Brown at the time, reported seeing him running away. What is known for certain is that when the last bullet struck Brown, he fell forward into the street and was soon after pronounced dead by paramedics.

As a crowd gathered around the scene, people began to take pictures and videos of Brown's body. The photos soon spread on social media, and people reacted quickly with anger and heartbreak. Theories ran wild, and false information began to spread alongside the facts about the incident. "Ferguson police just executed an unarmed 17yr old boy that was walking to the store. Shot him 10 times smh," was written in a Twitter post shortly after the incident.[8] Some speculated that Brown's body was left on the street for several hours as a warning to others, a claim disputed by former Ferguson chief of police Thomas Jackson in his book *Policing Ferguson, Policing America.* As the news went viral, anger spread, and the feeling was all too familiar. The nation was still on edge from Trayvon Martin's murder in 2012 and the acquittal of George Zimmerman in 2013. In addition, just a few weeks before Brown's death, Eric Garner of Staten Island, New York, a black man, died from being placed in a choke hold by police. They had confronted him for the minor crime of selling loose cigarettes—cigarettes that are sold individually to avoid paying city taxes.

Brown was young and unarmed. Why did the officer respond with deadly force when he could have simply taken Brown into custody?

Protests and rallies swept through many American cities in response to the killings of Brown and other African Americans. Protesters sought to bring attention to injustice.

People wanted answers to these questions and for the officer to face charges. They wanted assurances that their own children were going to be safe. "There is no other people on Earth that I love more than my children," said Ferguson resident Amy Hunter to a gathered crowd in the week following Brown's death. "And I would really like to stop being afraid every time they leave my house."[9] Others believed that it was more important to stand by law enforcement and trust Wilson's account of the event. This ignited debate on social media between

Wilson's supporters and those who wanted to see him punished for the killing.

The Saint Louis Police held a press conference on August 10, the day after the shooting, in which they said that Brown was killed because he reached for Wilson's gun. In response, Ferguson residents and supporters gathered in peaceful protest outside of the Ferguson police department. Across the country, similar protests cropped up. In Ferguson, the protests eventually turned violent, resulting in looting, rumors of gunshots, and riots. Riots continued into the next day and the day after, and the National Guard was called in to help calm the situation. Missouri governor Jay Nixon called for a curfew to keep people off the streets. Only after US attorney general Eric Holder flew to Ferguson to meet with Brown's family on August 20 did the riots cease.

A few months after the shooting, on November 24, 2014, the Saint Louis County prosecutor, Robert McCulloch, made the announcement that Wilson would not be facing charges for the incident. The reaction online and in Ferguson was almost immediate. People marched in protest, and some protests again led to violence. In online reactions, many people were angry at the outbreak of violence and resulting property damage. Others were quick to defend protesters, noting that only a few individuals, rather than the widespread protest movement, were responsible for the problems.

To some, Brown's death was an isolated tragic incident. But others saw it as part of a long-term pattern of mistreatment of black Americans by police. In Missouri, black drivers are 85 percent more likely than whites to be pulled over. They are also 51 percent more likely to be searched during a traffic stop, even though, according to a Missouri report on vehicle stops, white people are more likely to be found with illegal drugs. Police are also more likely to use deadly

Colin Kaepernick Takes a Knee

Colin Kaepernick's protest started out small and went relatively unnoticed at first. The San Francisco 49ers quarterback simply remained seated while the national anthem played at the beginning of the first two preseason games of the 2016 season. It wasn't until the 49ers played their third preseason game on August 26 that people took notice. When asked about his actions, Kaepernick, who is mixed race, told the press that he was sitting to protest police brutality and the oppression of people of color in the United States.

Former Seattle Seahawks player and army veteran Nate Boyer was watching this protest and got in touch with Kaepernick to make a suggestion. In order to show respect for members of the military, Boyer recommended that Kaepernick take a knee rather than sitting. On September 1, Kaepernick took a knee for the first time, accompanied by 49ers safety Eric Reid. Across the NFL, other players began to kneel during the anthem, while others remained standing but raised a fist. But not everyone was on board with Kaepernick's protest. Many angry 49ers fans burned their Kaepernick jerseys and shared angry comments online, believing that the protest was disrespecting the anthem and the nation.

In March 2017, Colin Kaepernick opted out of a contract and became a free agent, eligible to be signed by another team. But no team opted to hire him during the 2017 season. Many suspected that this was due to his political activism, rather than his abilities as a player.

force against black individuals. Various studies have found that black men between the ages of fifteen and thirty-four are between nine and sixteen times more likely to be killed by police than other people. These imbalances in policing are reflected in the prison population, with black people five times more likely than whites to be incarcerated. Black people made up 33 percent of the prison population in 2016, despite only accounting for 12 percent of the US population.

As people in the black community try to speak out about these disparities, they often face racist backlash online. Many who read their comments misinterpret questions about police violence as opposition to law enforcement, flipping the narrative to paint police as victims of criminal misbehavior. Black Lives Matter activism in the wake of the Brown shooting was met with chants of "Blue Lives Matter," an attempt to shift the focus toward police, who often wear blue uniforms.[10] Others responded with the chant "All Lives Matter," again drawing the focus away from the specific problem of violence against black people. Many in the black community continue to struggle as they feel their concerns have gone unaddressed, particularly by the government.

White Supremacy in the Trump Era

On June 16, 2015, businessman and TV personality Donald Trump announced that he would be running for president in 2016. In his comments that day to gathered supporters at Trump Tower, his skyscraper in New York City, he said of immigration issues, "When Mexico sends its people, they're not sending their best. . . . They're bringing drugs. They're bringing crime. They're rapists. And some, I assume, are good people."[11] Trump almost immediately faced backlash online for his comments, which many considered to be

Many people felt Trump failed to strongly condemn his racist and bigoted supporters during the presidential campaign. These criticisms became even louder during his presidency.

racist. He doubled down on his position, frequently talking about how gang members and terrorists sought to illegally enter the United States. Trump called for a crackdown on undocumented immigrants, those who have entered the United States outside of the official legal channels or who have remained in the country after their original paperwork has expired. Many such people flee to the United States to escape violence in their home countries. He also proclaimed repeatedly that he would order the construction of a wall along the US border with Mexico.

Many voters liked Trump's brash way of speaking. They liked his stance on immigration. Some were easily able to link his statements and policies to their own biases against people of color. These ideas spread particularly widely online. Groups professing white supremacy became more visible on online forums and social media. In 2000, there were 602 documented hate groups operating in the United States. By 2018, that number had increased to 953.

> **"They're bringing drugs. They're bringing crime. They're rapists. And some, I assume, are good people."**[11]
>
> *– Donald Trump in his presidential campaign announcement speech, June 16, 2015*

After Trump won the presidential election and was sworn into office in January 2017, many immigrants became concerned for their safety and the safety of their families. Undocumented individuals felt more at risk for deportation by Immigration and Customs Enforcement (ICE), a government agency founded in 2003 to closely monitor those who are undocumented. During the Obama administration, ICE was tasked with deporting people guilty of crimes other than lacking documentation, but when Trump became president, his administration pushed ICE to remove anyone residing in the United States illegally. Additionally, people seeking asylum in the United States in early 2018 found themselves detained by US Customs and Border Protection. Parents were separated from their children at the border and often struggled to regain custody once released. These government actions were frightening for many Americans who view the United States as a symbol of freedom.

In August 2017, an outburst of racism found its way onto the front page of newspapers around the country. More than 200 white

supremacists marched in a Friday night August rally at the campus
of the University of Virginia in Charlottesville. They carried torches

Bree Newsome Captures the Flag

It was June 27, 2015, and Bree Newsome needed to do something.
Just ten days prior, nine black parishioners at a church in downtown
Charleston, South Carolina, were gunned down by a white supremacist
during a prayer meeting. Looking up at the Confederate flag on display in
front of the State House in Columbia, South Carolina, Newsome couldn't
wait for other forms of protest to do their job. Instead, she climbed the
flagpole and removed the Confederate flag herself. "We removed the
flag today because we can't wait any longer. We can't continue like this
another day."[1] The Confederate flag has long been regarded as a symbol
of the southern United States, and many white Southerners believe that it
represents their heritage and the heritage of their ancestors who fought on
the side of the Confederacy during the Civil War. Others consider it to be
a symbol of hate, particularly against African Americans, many of whose
ancestors were enslaved in the South.

After the incident, South Carolina governor Nikki Haley called for the
flag's permanent removal, saying that the flag "never should have been
there." She said, "These grounds are a place that everybody should feel a
part of. What I realized now more than ever is people were driving by and
felt hurt and pain. No one should feel pain."[2] Haley suggested that the flag
be placed in a museum instead.

Newsome and her friend James Tyson were arrested and charged
with defacing a monument, but charges were dropped. The Confederate
flag no longer flies outside of the South Carolina State House.

1. Quoted in Brent Staples, "Bree Newsome Removes a Symbol of Hate," New York
Times, June 29, 2015. www.nytimes.com.

2. Quoted in Eugene Scott, "Nikki Haley: Confederate Flag 'Should Have Never Been
There,'" CNN, July 10, 2015. www.cnn.com.

and chanted racist slogans. Antiracist counterprotesters clashed with them. The police finally intervened, and people on both sides suffered injuries. The next day, another round of protests and counterprotests erupted into more widespread violence. Events turned deadly when one white supremacist intentionally rammed his car into a crowd of counterprotesters, killing one woman. On the same day, two police officers who had been monitoring the events from a helicopter died when their aircraft crashed.

Trump made public remarks in response to the events in Charlottesville. He said, "We condemn in the strongest possible terms this egregious display of hatred, bigotry and violence on many sides, on many sides."[12] People took issue with Trump's phrase "on many sides." He seemed to be drawing an equivalency between the racist protesters and those who were standing against racism. At a later press conference, Trump went further, stating, "You had some very bad people in that group, but you also had people that were very fine people, on both sides."[13] Public figures from both major political parties condemned his remarks.

America remains on unstable ground when it comes to issues of race, but many hope that education and an antiracism narrative from the government will help to ease some of the concerns. Ibram X. Kendi, director of the Antiracist Research and Policy Center at American University, says, "There has not been a society-wide and intensive challenge to racist ideas in the US."[14] He and many other antiracism experts agree that one of the most important antidotes to racism in America is to challenge racist ideas and realign people's way of thinking.

Violence Against Muslims

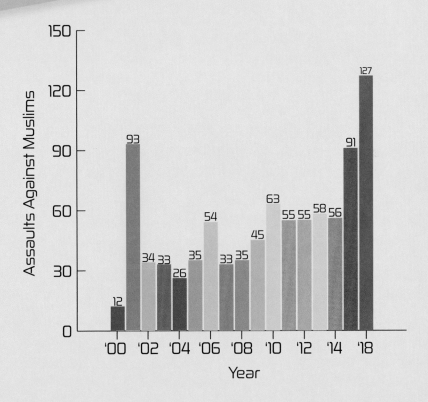

The number of assaults against Muslims in the United States shot dramatically upward following the terrorist attacks of September 11, 2001. The number fell the following year, though it gradually trended upward over the next decade. In 2015 and 2016, it again began to rise sharply. These statistics come from the FBI. The FBI notes that local law enforcement agencies voluntarily provide this data, so some agencies do not. This suggests the true figures are likely to be higher.

Katayoun Kishi, "Assaults Against Muslims in U.S. Surpass 2001 Level," Pew Research Center, November 15, 2017. www.pewresearch.org.

Chapter 2

How Have Women's Rights Changed in America?

August 18, 1920, was a momentous day for American women. This was when the Nineteenth Amendment to the Constitution was ratified, finally granting women the right to vote in elections. But this right was not easily won. The women's rights movement had a milestone moment more than seventy years earlier, at the 1848 Seneca Falls Convention in New York.

The convention was attended by around 300 people, both men and women. Lucretia Mott, a Quaker and abolitionist, addressed the assembly, as did Frederick Douglass, who believed that women's rights went hand in hand with human rights, particularly in the case of slavery, which was still legal at the time. "All that distinguishes man as an intelligent and accountable being," Douglass said in his address, "is equally true of woman; and if that government is only just which governs by the free consent of the governed, there can be no reason in the world for denying to woman the exercise of the elective franchise, or a hand in making and administering the laws of the land."[15] This convention and the words spoken there would become important in the struggle for women's rights. The event went down in history as a turning point for women.

Voting rights were only one part of the fight for women's rights, however. As the twentieth century rolled on, women's rights activists moved on to other issues. The first birth control clinic had opened in 1916, giving women control over their own reproductive choices for the first time in American history. The first hormonal birth control pill was approved by the Food and Drug Administration in 1960, setting off what would become known as the "sexual revolution" and a new wave of feminism. Women also fought for equal pay and representation in government and against sexual and domestic violence, issues that had been frequently overlooked as "private concerns" in the past.

> **"All that distinguishes man as an intelligent and accountable being is equally true of woman."[15]**
>
> *– Frederick Douglass addressing the Seneca Falls Convention, 1848*

Today, women continue to fight for the right to control their reproductive choices, hold the same jobs as men and receive equal pay, be heard in cases of domestic and sexual violence, and be elected to positions in government. Women of color fight for the same things, but their challenges are compounded by the racial discrimination that has been ingrained in American society. Hard-won achievements have been made, but women in the twenty-first century continue to face a wide variety of challenges in these arenas.

Hillary Clinton and Women in Politics

On November 6, 1931, Senator Thaddeus Caraway passed away, leaving many in his home state of Arkansas wondering who would take over his seat in the Senate. Days after his funeral, Harvey Parnell, Arkansas's governor, appointed his widow, Hattie Wyatt Caraway, to the seat. Just a year later, she was up for reelection and won, becoming the first woman to be elected senator in the United States. Shirley Chisholm became the first African American woman elected to Congress in 1968. These and other women opened the door to women stepping into roles in government.

But could a woman ever become president of the United States? This was a question on a lot of minds when, in 1984, US Representative Geraldine Ferraro was selected as Democratic presidential candidate Walter Mondale's running mate. Mondale and Ferraro lost the election of 1984, and another woman would not find herself on a major party ticket again until 2008, when Sarah Palin, then governor of Alaska, was selected as Republican senator John McCain's running mate in the presidential race. Palin faced many of the same sexist double standards that Ferraro had almost twenty-five years before. The mother of five children, Palin dealt with comments that she was neglecting her duties in order to pursue her career. McCain and Palin's bid for the presidency was unsuccessful.

Hillary Clinton, former first lady, former senator, and former secretary of state, would be the next woman on a presidential ticket, this time as a candidate for the presidency itself. After losing the Democratic nomination to Barack Obama in 2008, Clinton was a favorite for the nomination in 2016, facing Senator Bernie Sanders in the Democratic primaries. Clinton had been in the public eye since late 1991, when her husband, Bill Clinton, announced he would be entering the presidential race. During the 1992 campaign, Hillary Clinton faced criticism of her hairstyle, clothing, and choice to be a working mom. Former president Richard Nixon said in an interview

In 2016, Hillary Clinton became the first female candidate nominated by a major party for president. Though she lost the election, her campaign helped inspire a new wave of young women to run for office.

about Clinton, "If the wife comes through as being too strong and too intelligent, it makes the husband look like a wimp."[16]

In her own bid for the presidency, Clinton continued to struggle against sexist commentary and speculation. In January 2008, during a sit-down with locals at a diner in Portsmouth, New Hampshire, a voter named Marianne Pernold Young asked Clinton how she stayed upbeat on the campaign trail. Clinton responded emotionally, with tears in her eyes: "Some of us just put ourselves out there and do this against some pretty difficult odds. And we do it, each one of us, because we care about our country."[17]

But it was the tears and not her answer that captured the notice of the media. Many speculated that Clinton's show of emotion was a manipulation tool to garner support. "She pretended to cry," said political analyst William Kristol to Fox News.[18] Emotions are often considered a feminine characteristic and frowned upon, especially for women in positions of power. According to an article by Maureen Dowd of the *New York Times,* after the incident in New Hampshire took place, she overheard a male coworker say, "Is this how she'll talk to [North Korean dictator] Kim Jong-il?"[19]

> **"Some of us just put ourselves out there and do this against some pretty difficult odds. And we do it, each one of us, because we care about our country."[17]**
>
> *– Hillary Clinton during the 2008 Democratic presidential primary campaign*

Female candidates have historically received less support because of their gender. According to a poll from 1937, only 33 percent of Americans said they would vote for a woman running for president. In 2015, the result was 92 percent, but gender bias still plays a role in how decisions are made. Throughout most of American history, women were limited to making a home and being a mother. So when women run for office, voters often respond more positively to a candidate who seems to embody that role than to one who focuses on her education and chooses to work outside of the home. There's also an emphasis placed on attractiveness. Clinton is known for wearing pantsuits. During her run for the vice presidency in 2008, Palin was more commonly seen wearing knee-length skirts and high heels, making her appear more feminine and therefore more attractive to many male voters. In addition to having to be qualified and act professional in public, which is the expectation for any candidate for political office, female candidates are also expected to be conventionally attractive.

In 2016, Clinton won the primary and went on to face the Republican nominee, Donald Trump, in the general election. Many 2016 voters liked Trump. He had a brash speaking style and a conservative agenda toward issues like taxation and immigration. Some felt that Clinton, despite her years of experience in politics, was still not ready to be president. Many people believed that at least some of the opposition to her was sexist in nature. Though Clinton won the popular vote by a substantial margin, Trump won slim majorities in the states needed to win him the presidency in the Electoral College. He became president in January 2017.

But women were not going to have their concerns go unheard and unacknowledged. The day after Trump's inauguration, January 21, 2017, women and their allies gathered in protest across the United States—and in other parts of the world as well. An estimated 1 million women marched on Washington, DC. This would be one of the biggest, most widespread protests in American history.

#MeToo

Early in the day on October 10, 2017, Twitter was buzzing more than usual. Rumor had it that journalist Ronan Farrow had written a controversial article for the *New Yorker,* accusing movie producer Harvey Weinstein of sexual assault against multiple women. The article was soon posted online, validating these rumors and changing the movie industry, and the world, forever.

Widespread inappropriate behavior against women and girls has long been an open secret in the film industry. In old Hollywood, women were often expected to assent to sexual advances with the

Vast crowds of women marched on Washington, DC, in January 2017. Many were motivated by Trump's history of derogatory statements and actions toward women.

understanding that if they didn't, their careers would be over. While many industries changed with the times and worked to create safe spaces for women, the film industry continued to uphold sexist traditions. According to a *USA Today* poll, 94 percent of women in the entertainment industry say that they've been the victim of sexual assault or harassment. The *New Yorker* article finally brought this kind of behavior into the spotlight. Actresses including Ashley Judd, Rose McGowan, Salma Hayek, Gwyneth Paltrow, and many others stepped forward to share their experiences of sexual misconduct by Weinstein.

Weinstein wasn't alone in the spotlight for long. The article opened a floodgate of accusations against producers, directors, actors, and other men in the film industry. And the accusers weren't always women. Several days after the Weinstein accusations came to light, actor Anthony Rapp shared that actor Kevin Spacey had made sexual advances toward him when he was fourteen, and additional accusations against the actor soon followed. As a result, Spacey lost his role in the Netflix drama *House of Cards.* Weinstein was eventually arrested on May 25, 2018, and charged with rape.

Victims felt like they were finally being heard. Emboldened by those coming forward with stories of sexual harassment and assault, others added their voices. Years earlier, in 2006, an activist named Tarana Burke had started a movement and named it Me Too. Burke had herself been the victim of sexual violence and wanted to connect with survivors like herself. "I knew when you exchange empathy with somebody, there's an immediate connection you make with a person by saying 'me too,'" she said in an interview.[20]

> **"I knew when you exchange empathy with somebody, there's an immediate connection you make with a person by saying 'me too.'"[20]**
>
> *–Activist Tarana Burke*

The movement was all about victims sharing their stories to help other victims of similar acts of sexual violence. In the wake of the accusations against Harvey Weinstein, actress Alyssa Milano asked that her followers share their own stories using the hashtag #MeToo, and they did. The movement went viral across social media. Within twenty-four hours, there were 12 million posts using the #MeToo hashtag.

Not all responses were positive, however. Some people saw #MeToo as an opportunity for false accusations to be made and accepted without question. They felt that it changed the dynamic of a social environment, where, for instance, people felt afraid of complimenting a woman's clothing because they might be accused of inappropriate behavior. "You have to tiptoe around people. You can't even be yourself," said a female member of a focus group conducted by Vox Media.[21] And what then happened to those who were accused? Many men who had faced accusations had seen their careers destroyed and lost the trust of loved ones and friends.

Ultimately, the #MeToo movement changed the way that people think and talk about sexual violence, which has always been prevalent in American society but has rarely been talked about. It channeled

Spaces for Women in Video Game Development

Video game developer Zoe Quinn was on a mission. She was trying to bring attention to a new game she was developing called *Depression Quest*. The game was about her struggles with mental health. There was a lot of backlash online in response to the game. Some people felt much of the criticism came down to Quinn being a woman in the male-dominated video game industry. Quinn was soon inundated with death threats and harassment. This harassment was heightened when an ex-boyfriend of Quinn's posted an account of their relationship online, implying that Quinn had been unfaithful to him with men who worked in the video game industry in order to gain some good publicity for her game. Her address and phone number were posted online, and soon the death threats became so overwhelming that Quinn had to move out of her home and live with friends. A similar series of events happened to journalist Anita Sarkeesian, who has critically analyzed the treatment of female characters in games. This backlash against women in gaming became known as Gamergate.

The #MeToo movement has spread not just around the United States, but to countries across the globe. South Korean protesters marched as part of the movement in August 2018.

social media toward positive change and outreach to victims, and it helped to chip away at the continuing impact of sexual violence and harassment in the entertainment industry and throughout American society.

Roe v. Wade Today

The 1973 Supreme Court ruling *Roe v. Wade* made abortion legal throughout the United States. Before then, women with unwanted pregnancies were faced with a choice: carry the pregnancy to term or pay someone to perform an illegal abortion. Some women who couldn't afford to pay someone for an abortion tried to end their unwanted pregnancies at home, often using unsterilized tools like knitting needles and coat hangers. This procedure could easily go wrong, resulting in infection and even death. In her book *This Common Secret: My Journey as an Abortion Doctor*, Susan Wicklund shares a story of breaking the news to her grandmother that she performed abortions. She expected her grandmother to be disappointed in her, but instead her grandmother shared her own story of helping a friend abort a pregnancy seventy-two years before. The friend bled to death as a result, and the grandmother was still wracked with guilt. "I know exactly what kind of work you do, and it is a good thing," Wicklund's grandmother said.[22]

Abortion, however, is an extremely controversial procedure and one that has divided the nation for more than a century. Those who oppose abortion do so because the procedure results in the death of the fetus. They feel that abortion is therefore simply murder. People who support abortion rights want women to be free to make their own reproductive decisions. Of the 123 million pregnancies that occur each year across the globe, 87 million of these are unintended, according to the World Health Organization. Although unplanned pregnancies in the United States were going down by 2016, women still seek abortions. *Roe v. Wade* gave women access to legal and safe abortion for the first time in US history.

In its ruling, the Supreme Court decided that criminalizing abortion violated a woman's constitutional right to privacy, and the procedure became legal nationwide. States, however, could still set restrictions on abortion after a certain number of weeks. Safe, legal abortion saves the lives of pregnant women. Those who oppose abortion would like to see *Roe v. Wade* overturned, and supporters fear that would mean a return to a more dangerous time for women. Traditionally, the Republican Party has opposed the *Roe v. Wade* decision, and the Democratic Party has supported abortion rights.

Abortion has remained a deeply divisive women's rights issue for decades. In some cases these strong feelings have led to anti-abortion activists carrying out acts of violence.

Pregnancies are divided into three periods of time called trimesters. Abortions are most commonly performed in the first trimester. But second- and third-trimester abortions are sometimes necessary, and Kansas doctor George Tiller was one of the few abortion doctors in the country who would perform this type of procedure. On May 31, 2009, Tiller was attending church in his home town of Wichita, Kansas, when an anti-abortion protester named Scott Roeder confronted him with a gun and shot him once. Tiller died at the scene. This wasn't Tiller's first confrontation with protesters, or even the first time he had been shot. He had survived a shooting in 1993. This shooting and Tiller's death represented a struggle that had been going on for years.

Violence against doctors who perform abortions has long been an issue in the United States. One of the first reported arson fires at an abortion clinic happened in 1976. Since then, anti-abortion protesters have bombed clinics, sent letters containing poison, and committed acts of vandalism. On November 29, 2015, three people were shot and killed at a clinic in Colorado Springs, Colorado, bringing the number of deaths caused by anti-abortion extremists to eleven people since 1993. Violence and threats of violence against doctors and clinic employees has only increased. Threats like these almost doubled in 2017.

Additionally, the future of *Roe v. Wade* became uncertain in 2018, when Supreme Court justice Anthony Kennedy announced his retirement on June 27. Justices mostly aligned with Democrats had held a majority in the Supreme Court for fifty years, but the conservative President Trump was set to appoint a justice whose politics matched his own to succeed Kennedy. Many feared that a conservative majority could simply overturn the *Roe v. Wade* ruling if the right case came along. On July 9, Trump announced his nominee: federal judge Brett Kavanaugh. Many of Kavanaugh's past decisions showed him to be against abortion, giving him an edge among Republicans. Still, the Trump administration hoped to gain support for their pick in the Senate—whose job it is to confirm Supreme Court nominees—by promoting Kavanaugh as a friend of women. Kavanaugh has two daughters and a history of hiring female employees. However, the judge soon came under fire. Christine Blasey Ford, a college professor from California, sent an anonymous letter to Senator Dianne Feinstein alleging that when she was in high school she went to a party where Kavanaugh was also in attendance. Ford said that Kavanaugh and a friend, allegedly both intoxicated at the time, cornered her in an upstairs room at the party, pinned her down, and attempted to remove her clothing. Ford fought back and got away, but she hadn't forgotten the encounter. She was brought in to testify during Kavanaugh's confirmation hearing. But her account and similar allegations from two more women were not enough to dissuade the US Senate from confirming Kavanaugh. Many women and their allies were upset, not only because they feared for the future of *Roe v. Wade* and women's safety, but because they felt that Ford, like many victims of assault, had been pushed aside for the sake of politics.

The Truth About False Accusations

"It's a very scary time for young men in America," said President Donald Trump at the White House on October 2, 2018. Trump was referring to men's fears over allegations of sexual assault in a time when the #MeToo movement prompted many victims to come forward and share their stories. But studies show that, in reality, false accusations are rare. The percentage of false reports falls between 2 and 10 percent, based on different estimates.

But experts say these numbers may be inflated by law enforcement policies, sometimes including cases in which alleged victims report a crime and it is determined that no crime occurred. This is referred to as an unfounded report, which is different from a false accusation, in which the accuser is found to be lying. Women are often not believed, or are pressured into withdrawing an accusation, sometimes by police. According to a 2013 article in the *Baltimore Sun*, that city held the highest rate of unfounded rape cases, at 30 percent. But after Baltimore police went through special training and were asked to conduct fuller investigations, that number soon dropped to under 2 percent.

Quoted in Jeremy Diamond, "Trump Says It's 'A Very Scary Time for Young Men in America,'" CNN, October 2, 2018. www.cnn.com.

Chapter 3

How Have LGBTQ Rights Changed in America?

Living as a lesbian, gay, bisexual, transgender, or queer/questioning (LGBTQ) person today is different from the way it was in the past. Long before rainbow flags flew over Pride parades, friends gathered to watch a drag show, or people even felt safe simply holding hands publicly with a loved one, being LGBTQ was almost always a secret.

People often conflated homosexuality with perversion and sexual abuse, particularly against children. Certain sex acts were outlawed in many states. Those found guilty of such crimes could be stripped of professional licenses and lose their jobs and livelihood. In 1953, President Dwight D. Eisenhower issued Executive Order 10450, which banned gay men and women from working for the government. Government contractors were also ordered to fire suspected LGBTQ employees. This was justified under the belief that many LGBTQ people were more susceptible to blackmail by communists in a time when communism was making many Americans nervous. "We were just considered to be a threat to national security. So they wanted us gone," said air force veteran Helen James in 2018.[24] James was dishonorably discharged from the US Air Force for being gay in 1955 after investigators forced her to sign a statement dismissing her from

The Stonewall Inn became an iconic landmark in the history of LGBTQ rights. In 1969, LGBTQ people at the bar resisted police efforts to target them based on their sexuality.

the military under threat of the government outing her to her family. James signed, effectively ending her career and preventing her from collecting any benefits.

Transgender people, too, have long been subject to discrimination. In New York, an old law on the books banned farmers from wearing disguises while protesting against their landlords. This law was used to criminalize the wearing of clothing that didn't match a person's assigned sex at birth, so for many years transgender and nonbinary people who wore clothing to match their gender identity were often arrested and charged.

New York City, and in particular a bar called the Stonewall Inn, would become a key site in the history of the LGBTQ rights movement. The bar in Greenwich Village was a popular place to go to dance, drink, and wear whatever you wanted among likeminded

What It Means to Be a Girl Scout

The Girl Scout Mission has been to "build girls of courage, confidence, and character, who make the world a better place" since the group's founding in 1912.[1] But what it means to be a girl has changed in the twenty-first century, and the Girl Scouts have done their best to maintain a position of inclusivity. In 2012, a troop in Colorado allowed a seven-year-old transgender girl named Bobby Montoya to join their ranks after another troop leader denied her access. The local Girl Scout organization said in a statement to CNN, "If a child identifies as a girl and the child's family presents her as a girl, Girl Scouts of Colorado welcomes her as a Girl Scout."[2] Several conservative groups called for a boycott of the Girl Scouts in response. But the Girl Scouts continue to stand strong for all girls. Megan Ferland, CEO of the Girl Scouts of Western Washington, even turned down a $100,000 donation to the organization in 2015 when the donor insisted that the money secure an exclusion of trans scouts. "Girl Scouts is for every girl," said Ferland. "And every girl should have the opportunity to be a Girl Scout if she wants to."[3]

1. "Facts About Girl Scouts," Girl Scouts, n.d. www.girlscouts.org.

2. Quoted in Kata Hetter, "Girl Scouts Accepts Transgender Kid, Provokes Cookie Boycott," CNN, January 13, 2012. www.cnn.com.

3. Quoted in Sarah Larimer, "Girl Scouts Choose Transgender Girls Over $100,000 Donation," Washington Post, July 1, 2015. www.washingtonpost.com.

friends and allies. On June 28, 1969, in the early hours of the morning, the police launched a raid on the establishment.

Raids happened frequently at Stonewall—once a month, on average. If caught in a raid, people would be arrested, and their names would show up in the newspaper the next day. This had any number of consequences: loss of a job, being outed to friends and family, or worse. But the June 28 raid was different: people resisted. Many refused to show their IDs. Police vans pulled up outside, waiting to remove those who were under arrest. A crowd began to gather around, curious to watch the events unfold. The confrontation eventually turned violent, becoming a riot that would continue for the next six days. The next year, to commemorate the first day of the riots, the first Pride parade was held in New York City. One has been held every year since, and today Pride events take place in countries all over the world. The events at Stonewall became a foundational event in the history of social change for the LGBTQ community.

Prop 8 and Same-Sex Marriage

In 1970, a couple named Michael McConnell and Jack Baker attempted to get a marriage license in the state of Minnesota and were denied by the county clerk, Gerald Nelson, on the grounds that they were the same sex. The couple took Nelson to court, and it was decided by the state that they had no constitutional right to marry. The case went all the way to the Supreme Court, where their challenge to the decision was thrown out. While McConnell and Baker were not successful in their initial bid to marry, they did obtain a marriage license by legally changing one of their names to a more gender-neutral one. McConnell also legally adopted Baker so that he could ensure protections for his partner under the law. Their case

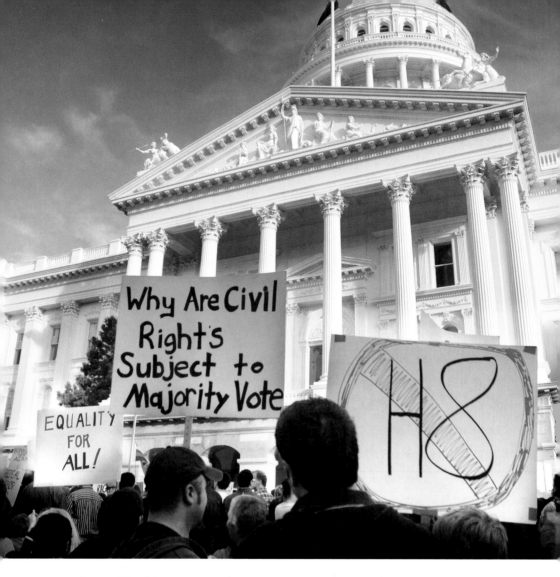

Proposition 8 became a major focal point for both supporters and opponents of same-sex marriage. Though it banned same-sex marriage in California, that ruling would be overturned less than a decade later.

brought the plight of many gay couples to the public eye for the first time.

The first state to legalize same-sex marriage was Massachusetts in 2004. Other states began to offer civil unions, legal arrangements that gave couples rights similar to those enjoyed by married couples. But this seemed, to many, like a cop-out. Similar wasn't equal.

A turning point for same-sex marriage came in 2008. In May of that year, the Supreme Court of California ruled that same-sex couples should have the right to marry. Couples streamed into the state to get their marriage licenses and finally make legal commitments to each other, often after decades of living together as a couple. But their joy was to be short-lived when Proposition 8, banning same-sex marriage in California, was approved by a slim majority of voters on Election Day that November. Prior to 2004, only three states had bans against same-sex marriage. By 2008, there were twenty-nine. This issue had grown in prominence. More people were talking about it. But conversely, by 2009, five states had legalized same-sex marriage.

Those who opposed same-sex marriage did so for a number of reasons, the largest being religious tradition. "Be fruitful and multiply" are words from Genesis, the first book in the Old Testament, which many took as a literal interpretation of what God wants for humanity: for couples to marry and have children.[25] Same-sex couples cannot have children through natural biological reproduction. Therefore, many believed that God would not support same-sex marriage. Others opposed same-sex marriage and relationships because they associated homosexuality with false stereotypes of promiscuity and perversion.

Prior to his 2008 presidential campaign, Barack Obama had remained on the fence about the issue of same-sex marriage. In 2004, when running for Senate in Illinois, he opposed the Defense of Marriage Act, which defined marriage as between one man and one woman only, but he was not yet in favor of same-sex marriage. But then in 2006, in his book *Audacity of Hope*, he said that he was "open to the possibility that my unwillingness to support gay marriage is misguided."[26] A major candidate standing in favor of same-sex marriage would be significant for those in the LGBTQ community, so they waited to see whether Obama's position would shift as his campaign, and later his presidency, got underway. In 2009, he signed the Matthew Shepard and James Byrd Jr. Hate Crimes Act, which made it easier for law enforcement to investigate and prosecute hate crimes, including those against LGBTQ people. In 2010, he signed a bill that repealed "Don't Ask, Don't Tell," a policy that kept gay and lesbian service members from being open about their sexual orientation. In 2012, Obama changed his official stance on same-sex marriage to one of support for its legality. Many Americans began to change their minds as well. A 2001 poll by the Pew Research Center showed support for same-sex marriage at 35 percent. But this figure rose significantly in the following decade. Views were changing, and supporters of same-sex marriage wanted to see laws change as well.

> **"The right to marry [was] inevitable. I always believed that. I just never thought it would take so long."[27]**
>
> – Jack Baker on the legalization of same-sex marriage, 2016

In 2010, a federal judge in California ruled that Proposition 8 violated the US Constitution. This was a huge win for LGBTQ rights, because now other states and other federal judges had precedent to overturn similar laws. In June 2015, the US Supreme Court ruled in the case of *Obergefell v. Hodges* that same-sex marriage bans were unconstitutional. This meant that same-sex marriage was now legal in all fifty states. After forty-five years of waiting, Michael McConnell and Jack Baker finally got to see other couples marry legally. "The right to marry [was] inevitable," said Jack Baker in 2016. "I always believed that. I just never thought it would take so long."[27]

Caitlyn Jenner and Trans Rights

"I used to think that I was broken. It wasn't until I was a freshman in high school that I found the word to describe the piece that was missing. I knew I was transgender, but for the first few months I had no idea how to accept myself as a boy so I started writing," said student Declan Nolan in a *New York Times* feature.[28]

People who are trans have a gender identity that differs from the sex they are assigned at birth. They may take steps to make the way they look and feel align more closely with the gender they identify with. This can mean dressing differently, having surgery that changes their body to be more masculine or more feminine, or taking hormones that help change their appearance. The challenges of living as a trans person—a term including but not limited to transgender, nonbinary, genderfluid, genderqueer, and intersex identities—are numerous. Basic documents that are used to identify a person, like a driver's license or passport, must be changed to match a chosen name or new appearance. Access to health care, and even finding a doctor who is accepting of a person's identity, can be a challenge. Family and friends might not accept a new identity, making a person feel alone or putting them at risk of depression or suicide. Jobs are harder to come by, leading to poverty.

The twenty-first century has brought with it a new wave of trans acceptance and visibility. More and more trans individuals are living

> **"I used to think that I was broken. It wasn't until I was a freshman in high school that I found the world to describe the piece that was missing."[28]**
>
> *– Student Declan Nolan, on realizing he was trans*

openly. In 2011, Chaz Bono, the son of pop singers Sonny Bono and Cher, was the first transgender man to appear on *Dancing with the Stars.* Model Andreja Pejic announced in 2014 that she wished to be

Trans Visibility On-screen

Orange Is the New Black, which debuted on streaming service Netflix in 2013, was a groundbreaking show for a number of reasons. It opened people's eyes to issues in the US prison system. It had a racially diverse cast of mostly women. Actress Laverne Cox quickly took center stage. Cox herself is trans, as was her character, Sophia Burset. In the past, trans characters were mostly played by cisgender actors. They were usually represented negatively, often as victims of crimes, as killers or villains, or as sex workers. Positive portrayals of trans individuals were very rare. Laverne Cox gave audiences a character who was complex and flawed and who struggled against a society that was stacked against trans women of color.

The show *Transparent* was also groundbreaking. Debuting on Amazon Prime in 2014, the show was developed by Jill Soloway and was based on the transition of Soloway's own parent, Carrie London. The show followed transgender woman Maura Pfefferman and her family as they came to accept Maura's transition and ultimately learn more about their own gender and sexual identities.

The film *Tangerine*, released in 2015, featured two transgender protagonists portrayed by trans actors. Trace Lysette, who played Shea on *Transparent*, said of the movie in an interview with OUT, "I saw *Tangerine* and I thought it was beautiful that we got to see trans women in leading roles. It was unprecedented and that in itself was a victory. I think visibly we're getting to a place—slowly but surely—where we need to be."

Quoted in Stacy Lambe, "An Oral History of Transgender Representation on Scripted TV," OUT, December 16, 2015. www.out.com.

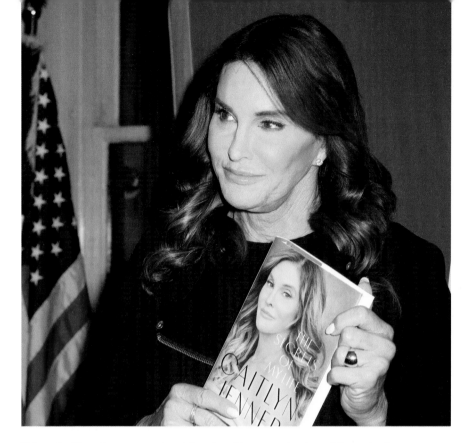

When Caitlyn Jenner went public about her gender transition, she became one of the most high-profile transgender public figures. In 2017 she published a memoir, *The Secrets of My Life*.

identified as a woman. Lana Wachowski, one half of the Wachowski siblings behind movies like *The Matrix*, publicly discussed her transition in 2012. Her sister, Lilly, came out in 2016. But probably the most prominent transition of the early twenty-first century was that of Caitlyn Jenner.

Jenner won gold for the decathlon in the 1976 Olympic Games and was lauded as a sports hero. Jenner later married Kris Kardashian, and the family skyrocketed to stardom with their reality TV show *Keeping Up with the Kardashians*, which launched on the E! Network in 2007. Jenner announced she was a trans woman in 2015. She appeared on the cover of *Vanity Fair* with the headline "Call me Caitlyn."[29] The Jenners divorced. This marked one of the first times that a high-profile celebrity had come out as trans. The world could no longer ignore trans issues. Whether or not the public was ready, the fight for trans visibility and acceptance had arrived.

One flashpoint in this fight came in public bathrooms. Bathrooms have traditionally been built to cater to only two genders: male and female. This can make life difficult, humiliating, and even dangerous for anyone whose sex assigned at birth does not match their gender identity. In response to the need for gender-neutral bathrooms, in 2012 and 2013, 150 university campuses installed such facilities, which anyone can use in relative safety and privacy. But costly renovations weren't possible in all public spaces. Therefore the question remained: Should birth sex or gender identity determine which bathroom you use?

Virginia high school student Gavin Grimm, who identifies as male, transitioned in 2014. He and his mother contacted Gloucester High School and were told by the principal that Gavin would be allowed to use the boys' bathroom. However, this decision was short-lived when community members complained. Some said that Gavin's presence might make other boys uncomfortable, even though Gavin used the bathroom for almost two months without any issues of this type. The school board then decided that Gavin should be required to use a separate gender-neutral bathroom. In response, Gavin brought a lawsuit against the school board. He was backed by the American Civil Liberties Union (ACLU). The case went all the way to the Supreme Court, thrusting Gavin into the spotlight and opening up one of the everyday struggles of trans people to public debate.

Around the country, many people saw an opportunity to address the issue head on. In Charlotte, North Carolina, in 2016, the city council approved an ordinance that would extend existing nondiscrimination protections to the LGBTQ community. This decision meant that Charlotte businesses—including restaurants, bars, stores, and car services—could no longer deny service to anyone based on sexual orientation or gender identity. This also allowed people to use the bathroom that aligned with their gender. In response, the North Carolina state government, with support from Governor Pat McCrory, quickly passed House Bill 2, which not only overturned the Charlotte ordinance but also banned any local statutes put in place to protect LGBTQ people from discrimination. "[I] firmly believe that in a middle school or high school a male should not be able to use the females' locker room or shower facility," said McCrory.[30] The bill would require people to use the bathroom that aligned with the sex on their birth certificate.

> **"[I] firmly believe that in a middle school or high school a male should not be able to use the females' locker room or shower facility."[30]**
>
> *–Pat McCrory, former governor of North Carolina*

Other states soon introduced similar legislation. By March 2017, there were fifteen such bills pending. Critics of these types of bills planned boycotts. Corporations and celebrities took strong stances in opposition. The major online payment company PayPal scrapped plans for building a facility in North Carolina. This business venture would have added $2.66 billion to the state's economy. Musician Ringo Starr canceled a concert that was to be held at a North Carolina amphitheater, costing the venue $33,000 in lost revenue. House Bill 2 was eventually repealed and replaced by House Bill 142, under new governor Roy Cooper. The new bill eliminates rules about bathroom use but still allows for discrimination against transgender people by businesses. Anti-trans legislation continues to be divisive for many Americans.

Gavin Grimm finally won the right to use the boys' bathroom in May 2018, when a federal judge ruled that the school board's bathroom policy subjected Grimm to sex discrimination. "I feel an incredible sense of relief," said Grimm in response to the decision.[31] Although Grimm had already headed to college, this court decision would be pivotal for similar cases in the future.

Pulse Nightclub and Violence Against LGBTQ People

Pulse was one of the most popular gay nightclubs in Orlando, Florida. More than 300 people were there in the early morning hours of June 12, 2016. Around 2:00 a.m., a man named Omar Mateen entered the club carrying an AR-15 rifle and a handgun and opened fire. Forty-nine people were killed in the attack, the largest US mass shooting up to that time. Mateen was soon shot by police. The shooter's father said that he believed his son's motivation stemmed from anger over seeing two men kissing. However, later evidence showed that the attack may have been motivated by political reasons related to US involvement in the Middle East. While the public might not ever understand Mateen's motivations, his actions led to some important conversations in the LGBTQ community and the media.

Much of the coverage of the attack was criticized by LGBTQ rights groups for not acknowledging that the shooting was a hate crime against members of the gay community. Not only that, ninety percent of the victims that night were Latino, compounding the likelihood that the crime was hate-based.

Hate crimes against LGBTQ people have long been an issue. They are the most targeted minority group in the United States, according to a 2016 article in the *New York Times*. In 2017 alone, fifty-two

Pulse nightclub was surrounded by memorials in the wake of the shooting there. The community rallied to remember those who died and support the victims and their families.

LGBTQ people were murdered in acts of violence determined to be hate crimes.

In the aftermath of the Orlando shooting, the LGBTQ community rallied as a number of new nonprofit organizations were founded to help meet the emotional and physical needs of the victims and their families and to stand up against gun violence. The group Gays Against Guns was founded in 2016 to fight back against the gun lobby with protests and street performances. Equality Florida raised more than $4 million through crowdfunding websites as donors all over the world contributed to the cause. This support demonstrated how people today are working to fight against intolerance.

Chapter 4

How Has the Role of Religion Changed in America?

Since the 1600s, when waves of colonists landed in what would one day become the United States, religion has played an important role in America. Europe was a hotbed of religious persecution in the sixteenth and seventeenth centuries. The New World, for many, meant a promise of religious freedom. They crossed the ocean to escape their oppressors. They established communities where they had more control over the rules, punishing those who stepped out of line and rewarding the most pious. They wrote about their beliefs and passed them down to their children and grandchildren in the hope that their teachings would survive into future generations. Attending church became the norm. In cities, churches grew in size and splendor. In rural areas, they were small and modest. But they were everywhere. Over the next few centuries, the church remained a town's hub of social activity. It was a gathering place in times of crisis. People relied on their faith and the churches that facilitated it.

But religion evolves, and so does society. Systems of belief collide and change alongside personal views and shifting trends in society. According to Leviticus 11:12 in the King James Bible, shellfish are unclean and it's a sin to eat them. But today many Christians eat

The desire for religious freedom was a major driver for many early European settlers who came to America. Religion continues to play a significant role in the lives of many Americans.

lobster and shrimp and crayfish without a second thought. Certain Christian denominations follow the Bible relatively loosely, while other sects call for strict adherence to what they believe is the word of God. And this dynamic is not limited to Christianity. Jews, Hindus, Muslims, Sikhs, Wiccans, and followers of all other systems of spiritual belief often interpret for themselves what faith means to them. The faithful often disagree on elements of belief and practice, sometimes to the point of starting wars, persecuting those who disagree, or discriminating against people.

Today the face of religion in America is changing dramatically. In 2007, 78.4 percent of Americans identified as Christian. Just seven years later, this number was down to 70.6 percent. The number of people identifying as unaffiliated or nonbelievers jumped from 16.1 percent to 22.8 percent. These and other changes in religion's place in American culture can have wide-ranging effects, intersecting with politics, women's rights, LGBTQ issues, and a variety of other facets of society.

Muslims and America

The tragedies of September 11, 2001, led to heightened anxiety for many Americans. After the attacks were attributed to Osama bin Laden and Muslim extremists, rumors swirled that Muslims both in the United States and abroad were celebrating. In reality, only one video, shot in Jerusalem, of a small group of Palestinians dancing was broadcast on the American news that day, and many have questioned whether the revelers were celebrating the attacks at all since the footage was shot earlier in the day. Still, the damage was done. Americans were afraid of another attack, and many people became suspicious of Muslims. In 2017, Rusul Alrubail of PBS News wrote about her own experiences on 9/11. Alrubail was in high school at the time. "Later that day on the bus going home, a student looked at my friend, my sister and me, who all wear a hijab [a head covering that some Muslim women wear], and said, 'Do you guys know what happened? I heard your people did it.'"[32]

Anti-Muslim and Anti-Arab sentiment was soon on the rise, along with distrust of anyone who looked like they might be Middle Eastern.

Just a few days after 9/11, a Sikh man named Balbir Singh Sodhi was shot to death outside of the gas station he owned by Frank Silva Roque. Roque believed that Sodhi was Muslim. That same day, Waqar Hasan, a Pakistani immigrant who lived in Dallas, Texas, was murdered in the store he owned by an attacker named Mark Stroman, who was not identified or caught immediately after the crime. Not quite a month later, Stroman also killed Vasudev Patel, an Indian man, in Mesquite, Texas. Stroman was arrested and later executed. In the United States, hate crimes against Muslims rose from twenty-eight in 2000 to 481 in 2001. Mosques, Muslim places of worship, were also under attack. On November 2, 2001, in Seattle, Washington, investigators attributed a fire in a local mosque to arson. Swastikas and ethnic slurs appeared on the exterior of a Muslim community center in Sterling, Virginia, on September 14, 2002. On May 10, 2010, in Jacksonville, Florida, a pipe bomb was detonated at an Islamic center.

"Later that day on the bus going home, a student looked at my friend, my sister and me, who all wear a hijab [a head covering that some Muslim women wear], and said, 'Do you guys know what happened? I heard your people did it.'"[32]

—Rusul Alrubail of PBS News on her experiences on 9/11

The numbers of anti-Muslim attacks were on the rise again in 2015, and many attributed this increase in part to the presidential campaign of Donald Trump. In 2015 Trump called for a ban against all Muslims entering the country, and he previously said that he would support building a database of all Muslims living in the United States. Between 2015 and 2016, there was an increase in anti-Muslim hate crimes of 19 percent. After Trump won the election, he followed through on a version of his pledge, signing an executive order on January 27, 2017, just a few days after taking office. Executive Order 13769 put a temporary hold on admission of refugees, as a well as a ninety-day ban on travelers from certain countries. The day after the ban went into effect, travelers from the seven countries listed in the order—Iran, Iraq, Syria, Yemen, Sudan, Libya, and Somalia—were not allowed to board planes to the United States, leaving many stranded in airports. Many of these travelers carried valid travel visas. Some had dual citizenship in the United States and another country. These people were denied entry as well.

Many Americans immediately fought back against the ban. At Kennedy Airport in New York City, a crowd gathered to protest after news spread of two Iraqi refugees being detained. Similar protests cropped up at other airports across the country. The ban was soon challenged by the courts. On February 3, Federal District Court judge James Robart issued a restraining order, which barred the travel ban from going into effect. On February 9, the 9th Circuit Court of Appeals in San Francisco ruled that the order violated due process, which is protected by the US Constitution. Trump responded in early March by revising the ban to only include six countries and allow an exemption for travelers carrying visas and green cards. A third travel ban, issued in September 2017, reintroduced much of the original order, but now included bans on travel from North Korea, Chad, and Venezuela. On June 26, 2018, the conservative majority of the Supreme Court upheld Trump's travel ban, citing concerns over national security.

Although many felt that the ban should be in place because of national security concerns, others believed that the ban constituted outright religious discrimination. Of the banned nations, only Venezuela is a predominantly Christian nation.

Protesters at airports around the country rallied against Trump's travel ban. Many interpreted his action as an implementation of his earlier suggestion to ban Muslims from entering the country.

The Rise of Religious Extremism

Extremism occurs when an individual or group so closely adheres to religious doctrine that anyone who doesn't share their beliefs becomes an enemy. Extremists often find elements of religious teachings that fit with their personal agenda and then use those teachings to cause harm to others. Islamist extremists, for example, take words from the Quran, their holy book, and interpret them to justify war and violence against Christians and Jews. Members of the KKK cite passages from the Bible that they believe justify their beliefs.

One of the most widely recognized religious extremist groups in the United States is the Westboro Baptist Church, based in Topeka, Kansas. The virulently anti-gay group often cites the Bible passage, "Thou shalt not lie with mankind as with womankind; it is abomination," to justify its actions.[33] People first took notice of Westboro when the group picketed the funeral of Matthew Shepard, a murdered gay teen, on October 16, 1998. Many Americans were outraged. In 2005, the group also began to picket funerals of US service members who had been killed in the wars in Afghanistan and Iraq, saying that God was punishing America for homosexuality by killing members of the military.

The First Amendment to the US Constitution promises the right to freedom of speech. However, the Constitution also protects anyone who stages a counterprotest. When high school running back Jake Bain of Ladue, Missouri, came out as gay in 2017, members of Westboro planned a protest. But when they arrived to protest, they were met with several of Bain's supporters who sang and chanted, and the Westboro members were soon drowned out. A similar counterprotest happened in 2016 after the mass shooting at Pulse nightclub in Orlando, Florida. After learning of Westboro Baptist Church's plans to picket victims' funerals, another group gathered to block mourners from hearing or seeing the Westboro members. People from nearby Orlando Shakespeare Theater dressed in white, wore large angel wings made out of fabric and PVC pipe, and stood in a line in front of the group from Westboro. "I don't have any money to give," said Jeannie Haskett, who helped to piece together the angel wings, "but I can spread love and I can spread hope."[34]

While Westboro Baptist Church has not committed any known acts of violence, there are individuals who do commit atrocities who call themselves Christians. Anti-abortion extremists calling themselves the Army of God have long taken credit for bombings of abortion clinics across the country. And in 2018, an extremist named

Mark Anthony Conditt was responsible for package bombs that killed two people and injured five in Austin, Texas.

Islamist groups are also a threat in America, and not just from members of these groups living overseas. Terrorist organizations often recruit online, appealing to young men, training them to plan attacks in their own countries, and giving them all the information they need to carry out those attacks. According to a 2018 report on NPR, 300

The Making of Equality House

The Westboro Baptist Church has an unlikely neighbor. Equality House stands directly across the street from the anti-gay church. Aaron Jackson, founder of the Planting Peace nonprofit organization, bought the house in 2013 and soon painted it with the colors of the pride flag as a symbol of standing against hate and for equality. Equality House is a gay rights center, and Jackson chose the location because of its proximity to Westboro. He sees the house as a "symbol of compassion, peace, and positive change."[1] Equality House even has a community garden and welcomes visitors to pick vegetables from it.

In the summer of 2013, a five-year-old girl named Jayden Sink set up a lemonade stand in the front yard. Jayden gave the lemonade for free but asked for $1 suggested donations. She raised $400 that day and an additional $26,500 with an online campaign for peace. That same summer Katie Short and Kimberly Kidwell were married on the house's front lawn. "We wanted to help play a role in bringing light to this critical issue," said Jackson.[2]

1. "Equality House," Planting Peace, n.d. www.plantingpeace.org.

2. Quoted in James Michael Nichols, "One Year of the Equality House Across the Street from the Westboro Baptist Church," Huffington Post, February 2, 2016. www.huffingtonpost.com.

Americans have left the country to join the Islamic State of Iraq and Syria (ISIS), a terrorist group based in the Middle East. Twelve have since returned to the United States after realizing that they would be relegated to household chores and have to endure unfavorable living conditions. Nine of these individuals were arrested. "I would see . . . people from all around the world leaving their countries and going to live in this state," said Mohamad Khweis, who fled the United States in 2015 to join ISIS. "It was kind of interesting."[35] Khweis immediately regretted his decision and attempted to escape three months later, when he was captured by Kurdish forces. He was later found guilty of supporting terrorism and sent to prison. ISIS has taken credit for a number of terrorist attacks, including the 2015 bombings and shootings in Paris. It continues to be a global threat.

Religion and Duty

When same-sex marriage became legal across the United States in 2015, many people were unhappy with the decision. Although the government's position on same-sex marriage had changed, this didn't change the minds of those who believed that God condemned homosexuality in the Bible. Many felt that accepting the government's decision over their own beliefs was wrong. One of these people was Kim Davis, the county clerk in Rowan County, Kentucky. County clerks are responsible for filing official paperwork on deaths, births, marriages, and other events within their jurisdiction that require specific personal documentation. Davis didn't agree with the decision to legalize same-sex marriage because of her religious beliefs, so when couples arrived to get marriage licenses, she refused. She didn't want her name to appear on these licenses, which was required of

The Activism of Malala Yousafzai

Malala Yousafzai was born in Pakistan in 1997. Her father, Ziauddin, ran a local girls' school, and Malala grew up excited about education and excelled in her studies. But thousands of miles away, things were happening that would change Malala's life forever.

The attacks of September 11, 2001, sent the world into a tailspin. The United States discovered that a religious militant group called the Taliban had harbored members of al-Qaeda. The Taliban ruled Afghanistan, and the United States invaded the country to attack the group. In response, the Taliban fled over the border into Pakistan. Soon, the Taliban's violence and extremist religious policies began to spread across parts of Pakistan. The Taliban decreed that women should stay confined to their homes, and if they did go out in public, they were required to wear a burqa and be accompanied by a male family member. Girls were also banned from going to school.

Malala and many of her classmates continued to attend school, often hiding their school bags in their shawls. Taliban forces began to destroy and close schools. When Malala was eleven, she began to speak out for her rights, sharing her blog anonymously with the BBC. Just a few years later, on October 9, 2012, Malala was on the bus heading home from school when gunmen climbed aboard. Malala was shot. She woke up several days later in a hospital in Birmingham, England. Since the attempt on her life, Malala has continued to speak out for women's education. She founded the Malala Fund, which invests in education programs. In 2014, Malala was awarded the Nobel Peace Prize. In her acceptance speech she said, "I tell my story, not because it is unique, but because it is not. It is the story of many girls."

Malala Yousafzai, "Nobel Lecture," Nobel Prize, December 10, 2014. www.nobelprize.org.

the county clerk at the time in the state of Kentucky. And she wasn't alone. Three of the 120 county clerks in Kentucky felt the same way.

Davis's supporters believed that she was doing the right thing by standing by her beliefs. People who disagreed felt that her actions violated the civil rights of those to whom she denied service. County clerks are government officials tasked with performing the duties of their office. Were Davis's beliefs more important than her job, which the people of Rowan County elected her to do? This was the question on the minds of many Americans. However, public opinion does not determine what's right. The courts make a decision based on the nation's laws. And that wasn't going to be easy in this case.

The Supreme Court's decision to overturn anti–same-sex marriage laws came down to the Fourteenth Amendment, which says, "nor shall any state deprive any person of life, liberty, or property, without due process of law."[36] This means that all Americans are subject to fair treatment by the courts, no matter their race, gender, or sexual orientation. Therefore, the Supreme Court believed that the right to marry fell under this amendment, and no state could deny another person a marriage license. Davis, however, felt that her choices should be protected by the First Amendment's promise of freedom of religion.

Kentucky's governor at the time, Steve Beshear, believed county clerks have a duty to the residents of their county and said they could do their jobs or resign. The courts agreed and said that by denying someone the right to acquire a marriage license, Davis was in violation of federal law. Said Davis, "If I resign, I lose my voice. Why should I quit a job that I love and I'm good at?"[37] Davis appealed, asking the courts to allow her office to be exempt from issuing marriage

> **"If I resign, I lose my voice. Why should I quit a job that I love and I'm good at?"[37]**
>
> – Kim Davis, county clerk in Rowan County, Kentucky

licenses. The case went to federal court, and it was decided once and for all that Davis had to perform the duties of her job.

But when the county clerk's office opened again, she continued to refuse to issue marriage licenses. Davis was sent to jail for five days. Finally, in 2016, a bill in the Kentucky senate was passed to remove the county clerk's name from marriage licenses. People continued to bring suits against Davis, prompting her in April 2018 to launch a case directing these individuals to instead sue the state of Kentucky. Later that year, Davis was voted out of office, defeated by Democratic candidate Elwood Caudill Jr.

Davis worked for the government, but what if someone who owns a business decides to deny service to an LGBTQ individual or group? This was the next big issue that came up. Jack Phillips owns a bakery near Denver, Colorado, and a gay couple, David Mullins and Charlie Craig, came into his shop in 2012 to ask him to bake a wedding cake for them. Phillips refused, saying that it violated his beliefs as a Christian. "I didn't want to use my artistic talents to create something that went against my Christian faith," said Phillips in 2017.[38] Mullins and Craig soon filed a complaint with the Colorado Civil Rights Commission, and the commission agreed with them based on a Colorado antidiscrimination law. Phillips then appealed the decision, citing that forcing him to bake a cake for a same-sex couple would violate his rights to freedom of speech and religion. The case eventually found its way to the US Supreme Court, and the court ruled in favor of Phillips. The decision found that the Colorado Civil Rights Commission hadn't treated Phillips fairly because of his religious beliefs. "Creative professionals who serve all people should be free to create art consistent with their convictions without the threat of government punishment," said Kristen Waggoner, the attorney who had represented Phillips.[39]

For the Sake of Social Change

Today, people continue to strive toward creating a better future. And positive social change is happening all the time. Black Lives Matter continues to gain momentum, with over 300,000 followers on Twitter. Many Americans also continue to show support for immigrants and refugees, even as the US government takes policy steps to reduce immigration and refugee admissions.

The #MeToo movement is growing, finally giving a voice to many women whose voices have been silenced in the past. And a record-breaking number of women were elected to Congress in 2018, including Alexandria Ocasio-Cortez, who became the youngest congresswoman in history.

While the LGBTQ community has seen its share of setbacks, overwhelmingly support for the community is growing. A 1985 survey asked members of the public if they would be upset if they discovered that their child was gay, and 64 percent said they would be. That percentage was down to 19 percent in 2013. Groups like the Trevor Project and Lambda Legal continue to advocate for LGBTQ people and educate others to help create a safe space for everyone.

Religion continues to divide Americans, but more and more people are learning and advocating for religious tolerance and understanding. Groups like Teaching Tolerance help give schools the tools for teaching children more about the world around them. The US Constitution supports religious freedom, and citizens continue to learn what that means for their own beliefs.

Moving toward attitudes of acceptance and equality can be difficult when many feel outnumbered and overshadowed by hate. Experts suggest that those who want to see positive social change should educate themselves on the issues and get involved in causes that affect them and those around them. "You can create a chapter

Young people from a wide variety of backgrounds are striving toward positive change in their communities. Together, they are working to create tomorrow's defining moments of social change.

of an existing organization (like Amnesty USA or STAND), or start an issue-based group of your own on anything from women's rights to AIDS awareness to anti-trafficking," suggests Natalie Jesionka of The Muse.[40] Experts also recommend voting or simply getting involved with the conversation if voting age is still a few years away. "Campaign issues arise because there are underlying problems to be solved. And anyone . . . anyone . . . with good ideas, creative solutions and the power of their convictions should jump in," says Illana Raia in an article on the *Huffington Post*.[41] People of any age can follow the latest news, write to their political leaders, speak out through their writing, or volunteer for a cause.

SOURCE NOTES

Introduction: Black Lives Matter in America

1. Quoted in Adam Weinstein, "The Trayvon Martin Killing, Explained," *Mother Jones*, March 18, 2012. www.motherjones.com.

2. Quoted in Amanda Sloane and Graham Winch, "Key Witness Recounts Trayvon Martin's Final Phone Call," *CNN*, June 27, 2013. www.cnn.com.

3. Quoted in Edward Upright and Zachary Fagenson, "Thousands Take to Streets to Protest Trayvon Martin Verdict," *Reuters*, July 30, 2013. www.reuters.com.

4. Quoted in Jessica Guynn, "Meet the Women Who Coined #BlackLivesMatter," *USA Today*, March 4, 2015. www.usatoday.com.

5. Jannell Ross, "How Black Lives Matter Moved from a Hashtag to a Real Political Force," *Washington Post*, August 19, 2015. www.washingtonpost.com.

Chapter 1: How Have Race Relations Changed in America?

6. Quoted in William Wan and Sarah Kaplan, "Why Are People Still Racist? What Science Says About America's Race Problem," *Washington Post*, August 14, 2017. www.washingtonpost.com.

7. George W. Bush, "'Islam Is Peace' Says President," *White House*, September 17, 2001. georgewbush-whitehouse.archives.gov.

8. Quoted in Thomas Jackson, *Policing Ferguson, Policing America*. New York: Skyhorse Publishing, 2017.

9. Quoted in Bill Chappell, "How People in Ferguson See the Police in Ferguson," *National Public Radio*, August 14, 2014. www.npr.org.

10. Radley Balko, "The 'Protect and Serve Act' Is Political Grandstanding Over a Nonexistent Problem—and It Could Cause Real Harm," *Washington Post*, May 11, 2018. www.washingtonpost.com.

11. "Full Text: Donald Trump Announces a Presidential Bid," *Washington Post*, June 16, 2015. www.washingtonpost.com.

12. Quoted in Ayesha Rascoe, "A Year After Charlottesville, Not Much Has Changed For Trump," *National Public Radio*, August 11, 2018. www.npr.org.

13. Quoted in Rascoe, "A Year After Charlottesville, Not Much Has Changed For Trump."

14. Quoted in Jamiles Lartey, "Oppression in America: 'To Root This Out We Need a Movement Against Racist Policies,'" *Guardian*, June 6, 2018. www.theguardian.com.

Chapter 2: How Have Women's Rights Changed in America?

15. Quoted in "Frederick Douglass," *National Park Service*, February 13, 2018. www.nps.gov.

16. Quoted in Andrew Prokop, "Richard Nixon's Incredibly Sexist Advice for Hillary Clinton in 1992," *Vox*, April 9, 2015. www.vox.com.

17. Quoted in Hendrik Hertzberg, "Second Those Emotions," *New Yorker*, January 21, 2008. www.newyorker.com.

18. Quoted in Hertzberg, "Second Those Emotions."

19. Maureen Dowd, "Can Hillary Cry Her Way Back to the White House?," *New York Times*, January 9, 2008. www.nytimes.com.

20. Quoted in Andrea García Giribet, "Tarana Burke: The Woman Behind Me Too," *Amnesty International*, August 21, 2018. www.amnesty.org.

21. Quoted in Anna North, "Why Women Are Worried About #MeToo," *Vox*, April 5, 2018. www.vox.com.

22. Quoted in Susan Wicklund and Alan Kesselheim, *This Common Secret: My Journey as an Abortion Doctor*. New York: PublicAffairs, 2007. pp. 90–91.

Chapter 3: How Have LGBTQ Rights Changed in America?

24. Quoted in Phoebe Judge, "Lavender Scare," *Criminal*, June 15, 2018. www.thisiscriminal.com.

25. "Genesis 1:18," *Bible Hub*, n.d. www.biblehub.com.

26. Quoted in Katy Steinmetz, "See Obama's 20-Year Evolution on LGBT Rights," *Time*, April 10, 2015. www.time.com.

27. Quoted in Julie Compton, "Gay Couple Pens Memoir After 45 Years of Marriage," *NBC News*, October 10, 2016. www.nbcnews.com.

28. Declan Nolan, "Transgender Lives: Your Stories," *New York Times*, October 19, 2018. www.nytimes.com.

29. Buzz Bissinger, "Caitlyn Jenner: The Full Story," *Vanity Fair*, June 25, 2015. www.vanityfair.com.

30. Quoted in Jim Morrill, "Here's What Ex-Gov. Pat McCrory Told a National Audience About HB2," *Charlotte Observer*, February 17, 2017. www.charlotteobserver.com.

31. Quoted in Matt Stevens, "Transgender Student in Bathroom Dispute Wins Court Ruling," *New York Times*, May 22, 2018. www.nytimes.com.

Chapter 4: How Has the Role of Religion Changed in America?

32. Rusul Alrubail, "Column: Why Educators Still Need to Talk About 9/11—and Islamophobia," *PBS*, September 11, 2017. www.pbs.org.

33. "Leviticus 18:22," *Bible Hub*, n.d. www.biblehub.com.

34. Quoted in Merrit Kennedy, "'Angels' from Orlando's Theater Community Guard Mourners from Protestors," *NPR*, June 19, 2018. www.npr.org.

35. Quoted in Mark Berman, "Young Men Left America to Join ISIS," *Washington Post*, February 8, 2018. www.washingtonpost.com.

36. "14th Amendment," *Legal Information Institute*, n.d. law.cornell.edu.

37. Hope Racine, "11 Kim Davis Quotes from Her 'Kelly File' Interview That Show She Doesn't Regret Going to Jail," *Bustle*, September 23, 2015. www.bustle.com.

38. Ariane de Vogue, "'It's Not About Cakes': Stakeholders Line Up on Both Sides of SCOTUS Religious Liberty Case," *CNN Politics*, December 4, 2017. www.cnn.com.

39. Quoted in Ariane de Vogue, "Supreme Court Rules for Colorado Baker in Same-Sex Wedding Cake Case," *CNN*, June 4, 2018. www.cnn.com.

40. Natalie Jesionka, "5 Ways to Get Involved with a Cause You Care About," *Muse*, October 30, 2018. www.themuse.com.

41. Illana Raia, "Too Young to Vote . . . But Old Enough to Care," *Huffington Post*, October 12, 2017. www.huffingtonpost.com.

FOR FURTHER RESEARCH

Books

Chimamanda Ngozi Adichie, *We Should All Be Feminists*. New York: Anchor Books, 2015.

Michael Bronski, *A Queer History of the United States*. Boston, MA: Beacon Press, 2011.

Jonathan Eig, *The Birth of the Pill: How Four Crusaders Reinvented Sex and Launched a Revolution*. New York: W. W. Norton & Company, 2014.

Christopher J. Lebron, *The Making of Black Lives Matter*. New York: Oxford University Press, 2017.

Malala Yousafzai, *I Am Malala: The Girl Who Stood Up for Education and Was Shot by the Taliban*. New York: Little Brown, 2013.

Internet Sources

Elijah Anderson, "This Is What It Feels Like to be Black in White Spaces," *Guardian*, June 9, 2018. www.theguardian.com.

Leila Fadel, "How Muslims, Often Misunderstood, Are Thriving in America," *National Geographic*, May 2018. www.nationalgeographic.com.

Erica L. Green, Katie Benner, and Robert Pear, "'Transgender' Could Be Defined Out of Existence Under Trump Administration," *New York Times*, October 21, 2018. www.nytimes.com.

Lindy West, "Why Is Fixing Sexism Women's Work?" *New York Times*, January 3, 2018. www.nytimes.com.

Websites

American Civil Liberties Union

www.aclu.org

The ACLU is an organization that defends Americans' rights under the Constitution. Its website offers information on its latest causes and what you can do to get involved.

Black Lives Matter

www.blacklivesmatter.com

The official site of the Black Lives Matter movement provides some important resources for the cause, as well as offering ways to help people get involved.

GLAAD

www.glaad.org

GLAAD works to promote understanding, acceptance, and equality for LGBTQ people in the United States.

Planned Parenthood

www.plannedparenthood.org

Planned Parenthood and its website are useful resources for learning more about sexual health and finding safe places that provide care.

Southern Poverty Law Center

www.splcenter.org

The Southern Poverty Law Center tracks hate groups in the United States and works to teach tolerance; the organization's website is a valuable source of information on the latest news and how to get involved.

INDEX

INDEX CONTINUED

IMAGE CREDITS

ABOUT THE AUTHOR

Bethany Bryan is a longtime editor and writer of nonfiction books for children and teens. She also edits kids' graphic novels and comics. She lives in Kansas City, Missouri.